"This book combines two things close to my heart: my recovery and praying the rosary. What a gift!"

PAT J.

"...made Scripture accessible in a way beautifully bridged with the familiar words of my 12-step program...a wonderfully simple way of getting closer to the God of your understanding."

MELISSA T.

"...inspirational words of wisdom for those recovering from life's addictions to help all of us reach our ultimate goal: peace and serenity."

LUCIA C.

"Now each time I "pray the rosary" something different happens. I have had many meaningful insights into my recovery: the need to work on various Steps...being overwhelmed with God's love for me and gratitude for His graces...enabling me to get out of myself and be receptive to another person's needs."

PATTI C.

The

Healing Rosary

**Rosary Meditations for Those
in Recovery from
Alcoholism and Addiction**

Mike D.

Resurrection Press
Mineola • New York

Nihil Obstat: Reverend Msgr. Lawrence Beeson, J.C.D., Censor Librorum

Imprimatur: ✠ Most Reverend Joseph L. Charron, C.PP.S.,
Bishop of Des Moines, June 23, 1998

First published in 1998 by Resurrection Press, Ltd.
P.O. Box 248, Williston Park, NY 11596
1-800-892-6657 (for free catalog)

Copyright © 1998 by MED

ISBN: 1-878718-40-1
Library of Congress Catalog Card Number: 97-75616

Cover photo and design: John Murello

Printed in the United States of America.

2   3   4   5   6   7   8   9   10

Acknowledgements

OF ALL THE THINGS I've intended to be, or pretended to be in life, an author was never one of them. Therefore, it is very important for me to acknowledge here that it was only by the power and love of God, the Author of all life, that the book you're now holding in your hands was ever written. I give my thanks to Him.

Also, I cannot possibly ignore the fact that I had the gentle help and inspiration of the Mother of Jesus, who in her quiet way did what she always does: magnifies the Lord.

Further, I give thanks to my wife, Lynn, who has never failed to give me her constant encouragement and help. I wish to give special thanks to my two favorite clergymen; Father Frank Chiodo, my parish priest, my friend, and pastor of the Basilica of St. John Catholic Church in Des Moines, Iowa; and to my good friend, Rev. Robert Elfvin, pastor of St. Luke's Episcopal Church in Des Moines. Both of these men of God did much to help pave the way for this work. I also received much needed help and encouragement from many good friends and family members, Steve and Eve Mahr, Rick C., Pat J., Greg K., Chris C., Lucia C., Patty C., Cathy Bates, Patty Brown and a long list of others who deserve to be mentioned here. My thanks to all of you.

MIKE D.

Contents

Foreword

WHEN I WAS ASKED TO WRITE a foreword for this book I immediately thought, "No, it's impossible. I'm too busy and behind on deadlines of my own." But then I remembered I always wanted to write something for A.A. members. I've been profiting by public A.A. meetings for forty years. I've been sending people to 12-step programs of all kinds for twenty-five years and I've never had anything stronger to drink than a glass of wine. I often joke with "members of the Guild" by telling them that I founded *Alaschlep* — an organization of people who would have made great alcoholics but they were too schleppy to ever get started. Seriously, I have often used the Twelve Steps and Traditions to clean out my own brain. So this book presented a chance to pay off a debt to Bill W. and to all of his spiritual descendants.

At this writing I've never met the author. I don't know his real name but I was both impressed and moved by his understanding of the method of prayer used in the rosary. He has it down very well. Even though he has chosen some other mysteries, the "healing mysteries," he calls them, he displays a fine grasp of the nature and purpose of repetitive prayer and he links, quite appropriately, the experience of Bill W. (*As Bill Sees It*, page 78) with this ancient devotion to the Mother of God. Repetitive prayer is known in almost every religion and, in fact, the use of beads for this kind of prayer is both ancient and widespread throughout humanity. Even Catholics who love the rosary of Our Lady will often use the same beads to recite other repetitive prayers like the Chaplet of Divine Mercy.

Mike writes with the authoritative experience of a recovering addict and at the same time with the faith of a believer. He is not a theologian and his experience of prayer should not be taken as a theological statement or an attempt to introduce a new rosary. His meditations are his own. They are used only to show a person seeking to pray the rosary what this form of meditation can do. Relating these meditations to the A.A. program will be much more helpful to a 12-step member than to someone unfamiliar with the spiritual journey of the recovering addict. But we members of Alaschlep can learn a great deal, too.

Many people use the rosary who are not Catholics. Some years ago a Methodist minister wrote a whole book on the benefits of the rosary. A great theologian, Msgr. Romano Guardini wrote of the rosary as "a spiritual place." I can only say that *The Healing Rosary* gave me some new insights even though I have prayed the rosary for six decades. In my own struggles to be a follower of Our Savior I have found the rosary to be a chain of prayer that linked me to Christ, to His mother and to that other reality which alone gives this life of struggle its meaning and its hope. I expect that this book will strengthen the prayer life and the convictions of anyone who reads it seriously and prayerfully.

Fr. Benedict J. Groeschel, C.F.R.

Introduction

THE TWELVE STEPS OF ALCOHOLICS ANONYMOUS are a pathway of healing that lead the suffering person to God, as that person understands God, for recovery from alcoholism and addiction. The only requirement for A.A. membership is a desire to stop drinking.

Two thousand years ago Jesus of Nazareth walked a pathway of healing. Each suffering person who came to him on his pathway, asking in faith for recovery, was healed, regardless of how that person understood him. Jesus' only requirement for healing was a desire to be healed.

This small booklet of meditations was written with the Twelve Steps of Alcoholics Anonymous as its foundation and the healing miracles of Jesus as its focus. Volumes have been written about these two subjects, yet they can both be summed up in these two simple words: God's love.

I am a recovering alcoholic, and it is by those two simple words, God's love, that I have remained continuously sober since January 24, 1988. In my desire to come closer to God through the Twelve Steps of A.A. and to improve my conscious contact with God through prayer and meditation at Step Eleven, I began to take particular notice of A.A.'s suggestion to return to the use of religious devotions "as never before." Meditation came very hard for me; in fact, this part of Step Eleven was nonexistent in my morning prayer time. I decided to give devotions a try because I needed something new in my prayer life. But I noted that the 12x12 had specifically spoken of "returning" to something. It soon became clear that it wasn't a matter of going out on a search to discover something new — it was only a matter of rediscovering something old.

As a Roman Catholic who had been away from the Church for a long time, it dawned on me that I had a devotion that is prayer and meditation combined and was readily available to me: the rosary. I hadn't prayed this devotion since my teen years, and certainly hadn't given it much thought in my adulthood. I was still considering all this when I realized that I had a rosary dangling from my dresser mirror which my Al-Anon wife (an Episcopalian) had given me as a birthday gift several years before I got sober. I hadn't paid much attention to it until then, but one morning I decided to take the A.A. suggestion; I took down the rosary, blew off the dust, poured myself a cup of coffee and began to pray, hoping it might help. When I finished, I had to admit that it did help; I felt better than I did before I started. So, I did the same thing the following morning. When I began to use it daily, I was surprised to discover that it affected my attitude and demeanor in a positive way. Now meditation was no longer some mysterious, complex concept for me — it was real. The rosary had effectively allowed me to quiet down inside and sit still long enough to "hear" the voice of God deep within; not necessarily an audible voice heard with my physical ears, but a voice we hear in that place in the heart where all words are ultimately heard. As I continued each day, I became aware of the feeling that God loved and treasured me. As an alcoholic who felt worthless and unlovable, this was new stuff for me. God's love wasn't new. It was my hearing it that was new, and it was this new "tool," the rosary, which had allowed me to finally listen and hear. I had returned to something very old, only to discover something brand new to me: a One-on-one encounter with God through meditation. It was a treasure found in my own backyard.

In the years of recovery since that time, I have had occasion to share my surprising experience of the rosary with many other alcoholics who, like me, also found meditation difficult and were looking for something that might help. I saw that if I could get benefit from it, anyone could do so — and denominations didn't matter. But one single event in my life has led me to handing this old/new devotion to countless recovering people:

In about the second or third year of my sobriety I was invited to an A.A. structured weekend retreat, which is held by other A.A. members in our area, at an Episcopal Church camp in a lovely rural, wooded setting. I had never been to one of these before, so I was curious and interested. I made a decision right then to go, and I invited two other A.A. friends, who also happen to be Catholic, to go along.

In the late afternoon on the second day of the retreat, my two friends and I were relaxing and enjoying the quiet of this place, when an odd thought popped into my head. I blurted out, "Hey you guys, since we're on a spiritual retreat, we ought to do something spiritual — let's go up to the chapel and pray the rosary."

They both thought it was a good idea, so the three of us ventured toward the small chapel only to find the doors locked until Sunday morning services. Not to be deterred, we walked down to the main lodge to obtain a key. There we found Patty C., one of the retreat leaders, chatting with a large group of other retreatants, and I requested the chapel key. As she handed it to me, she casually asked what we were going to do there. As discreetly as I could, I told her that we were on our way to pray the rosary.

What happened next changed things forever. She and all the others replied with wide-eyed enthusiasm; "The rosary? You're going to pray the rosary? Can we go too?"

I was very surprised because I knew that not one of them was Catholic. They came from a variety of Christian denominations, and some had no particular religious affiliation. As soon as I regained my composure I said, "Yes, of course you can!" So, up to the chapel we all went. Once we were settled, I spent a few minutes explaining the meditational nature of this devotion, then we all began to pray.

When we were finished, I was happily overwhelmed by the fact that three Catholic friends had first intended to pray the rosary, but instead, twenty-five men and women of diverse religious backgrounds had gathered in that little chapel and prayed the rosary together that day. It was a mystery I couldn't get out of my mind or my heart.

At the next retreat I brought thirty rosaries. Each of the retreatants eagerly picked one out and we all gathered in prayer and meditation again. Since that day, the rosary is a regular but optional part of this retreat for anyone who wants to join in.

Now, because they were non-Catholics I was a little mystified by it all at first, and wondered why they were so eager for this religious devotion which was so foreign to them. But I eventually realized that it had nothing to do with being Catholic or Protestant, or with having or not having a religious affiliation — it only had to do with being spiritually "hungry." They were all just like me. They, too, desired a deeper, closer One-on-one encounter with God. They wanted to do something that they had found difficult to do — just be still inside and open themselves to God in meditation.

In looking back it seems that what we thought was a locked chapel door to three people was really an open door to meditation for many more people. Their request, "Can we pray the rosary, too?" is still with me. This has been an important part of my Step Eleven journey, but my trek certainly hasn't ended there — it was just a beginning.

Because of the scriptural basis of the rosary, my attention was drawn back to the Bible, and I soon rediscovered the miracle healings and other kinds of miracles of Jesus that are described in the pages of the New Testament. I felt attracted to these Scripture accounts, and it occurred to me to use them in my rosary meditations. When I joined these awe-inspiring miracle healings from Scripture with the rosary in my morning meditations, it was like finding treasure in my own backyard once again. I was deeply affected in a most powerful and positive way. I felt that I had very much experienced the power of God through working the Steps. But now I began to encounter God as never before; I sensed the reality of the unconditional love and mercy of God. I saw myself as bad by nature, but God saw me as a good human being who is broken, and He stood eagerly waiting to heal all that is broken in me. Tears came for the first time in years.

The most fundamental, orthodox Judeo-Christian theology found in Scripture as well as the book, *Alcoholics Anonymous*, began to move from my head to the deepest part of my heart. The spiritual meanings of these two texts began to simply come alive and jump out at me.

I had to write down my thoughts and feelings, and this is how this booklet came to be written. At first it was only for me to use, but now I share it with you. What I desire to share is the greatest fruit that I derive from the rosary and the healing meditations — the reality of God's endless love. As you begin to pray and meditate upon these miracles, you will no doubt have your own thoughts, feelings, and experiences. I urge you to write them down.

Jesus hardly ever healed any two people exactly in the same way. Most often he dealt with each one as an individual person, according to his or her particular needs. I believe he still does this today. My written reflections are only meant to allow you to begin. Eventually what I have written you will put aside, and your own personal reflections will take their place — for these Scripture passages must become your own personal meditations, not mine. This is as it should be. You will encounter Jesus One-on-one, as I have encountered him. Jesus always healed by word and by touch, and he will speak to you, touch you, and heal you according to your needs, as he is still doing with me.

MIKE D.

About Miracles

THIS BOOKLET OF MEDITATIONS is about miracles because Alcoholics Anonymous is about miracles. We recovering alcoholics, who didn't necessarily spend much time thinking or talking about such things before, have come increasingly to believe in them for one simple reason: we've experienced them. As we further receive God's grace in recovery and share our experience of His grace with others, we often find ourselves speaking of miracles in A.A. meetings. With deep fervor and gratitude, we use the word often to describe many wonderful things, things that once were impossible but, by God's grace, are now a reality in our lives — especially, of course, our amazing recovery from alcoholism and addiction. God, we gratefully acknowledge, has miraculously done something that was humanly impossible for us.

Miracles. There is no more accurate word to describe the marvelous transformation that has taken place in our lives.

In moments of prayer and reflection, we may often begin to wonder why God sees fit to perform such miracles and wonders for the likes of us. Who among us can think of even one good reason why? When we think of our own experience of God's miracles and, at the same time, consider how far down we'd gone in our alcoholic sickness, we have to wonder, "Just how far would God go to save us from an alcoholic death?" Or maybe the real question is,

"How far did God go to save us?"

At first it would be easy to assume that there is no humanly conceivable answer to these thought-provoking spiritual questions. On the other hand, there might be something close to an answer we can understand, but to begin to find it, we must first realize the full extent of what a miracle is.

We in recovery have learned to turn to our trusty dictionaries to get a better understanding of the message in the Big Book. So your own dictionary will probably serve as the best source of information to begin to see what the word, miracle, actually means. I also discovered that a good definition can be found in religious dictionaries. While my old Webster's *New Collegiate* gives us this:

"MIRACLE: mir'a-k'l; (OF., fr. L. miraculum, fr. mirari to wonder.) 1. An event or effect in the physical world deviating from the known laws of nature, or transcending (going beyond, surpassing, exceeding) our knowledge of these laws; an extraordinary, anomalous, or abnormal event brought about by superhuman agency. 2. A wonder or wonderful thing; a marvel."

The *OSV Catholic Dictionary* defines it this way:

"MIRACLE (MIHR-uh-kuhl): The transcending of a law of nature, resulting in an unexplained occurrence that glorifies God. A miracle communicates God's will and His desire to save humanity."

Both dictionaries assign the word "miracle" only to those particular events in which we observe a radical departure from the laws of nature; a deviation from what is fundamentally known to be normal in nature.

There is another commonality: notice that both dictionaries assert that these are not accidental; they are willful, thoughtful, and deliberate. And they are always good.

Finally, both sources state that the Power who thoughtfully steps in, and deliberately commits these wonderful actions, is not any human power; it is super-human power — a Power greater than ourselves, God.

God created the universe and, in so doing, set in place his own natural laws which govern the order of all things. Everything in God's universe is bound by, subject to, and strictly obeys the laws of nature. All things, no matter how big or how small, must naturally operate and function within God's set boundaries, or natural laws, in order that they may play their specific, God-given role in His grand scheme of life.

According to His design, God has given humankind the ability to learn to manipulate and use many of those natural laws to good purpose. Throughout the ages the human race has continued to deepen its understanding of nature and its laws, as God intended. Science tells us that we must strictly obey the laws of nature in order to put them to effective use. For example, airplanes do not fly by defying the law of gravity — they fly only by rigorous adherence to the laws of aerodynamics. Even though God allows us to manipulate natural laws for human benefit, we cannot break these laws.

In Scripture, and especially in the New Testament, we see many extraordinary events that cause us to marvel at God. We see miracles of every variety — awesome, powerful happenings that took place in the lives of real people in human history. The four Gospels document thirty-six miracles that happened at the hands of Jesus himself, although they further tell us that he worked so many more wonders that they all couldn't possibly be counted and written down.

Whenever someone asked Jesus to heal them of a disease, that person was asking him to do something that was humanly impossible and beyond the laws of nature. When you think about it, such a request, no matter how humbly it was asked, goes way beyond anything reasonable. Nevertheless, we see that Jesus fulfilled each request on the spot — simply because a suffering human being was asking him.

Now, if human requests for healings seem extravagant, Jesus' willingness to comply with those requests is even more extravagant. In fact, we'd have to admit that all of these events are examples of pure extravagance from both the human and the divine side of each divine/human encounter.

But what do these wondrous events mean to us today?

As the Big Book tells us in the chapter "A Vision For You," God still does miracles for us today:

> *"The age of miracles is still with us."*
>
> (ALCOHOLICS ANONYMOUS, p. 153)

We know that the natural law of alcoholism, as with any terminal disease, is that it normally and naturally progresses until it systematically destroys a human being, first mentally, then spiritually, and finally physically.

Alcoholism naturally kills alcoholics.

But when we alcoholics come to realize that we are actually dying and admit that we can do nothing about it at all, when we desperately want to live, and we are willing to go so far as to surrender ourselves wholeheartedly to God's care and ask Him to stop the natural progression of this terminal disease, we are pleasantly surprised to find ourselves beginning to recover from the same disease that, only days before, was steadily advancing in its process of killing us.

Whenever we alcoholics today humbly approach God in this manner, we are really asking him to do the same thing that people asked Jesus to do two thousand years ago — we're asking God for a seemingly impossible healing.

We ask God, and the wondrous fact of Alcoholics Anonymous is that He gladly does it — just because we asked. And we who were once dying a slow and agonizing death from alcoholism and drug addiction know that this is a miracle. Moreover, it's just as amazing as any of the miracles found in Scripture.

But why does God do it?

Why would God be so extravagant with such small and unimportant people as us?

It is because God loves his people. God's healing wonders show us that God's love for us has no boundaries.

Now that's a pretty extravagant love, isn't it?

And God will reach out to heal us again and again because His love for us is boundless. God has never stopped loving any of his children from age to age — that's why "the age of miracles is still with us."

Now if God's love for us is boundless, this realization

raises another question for us to consider. It is a question about our own boundaries that we erect in our minds and hearts — a question about our faith in response to God's love:

If God's love has no boundaries, does my faith in God's love have any boundaries?

We often erect boundaries inside ourselves as a protection from the people, situations, and circumstances of life. We set these things in place to block out our emotional pain. Unfortunately, these barriers can block God out from us too.

God's love for us is boundless and extravagant, yet when God meets up with our boundaries, He respects our free will. Nevertheless, the very moment we make the slightest crack in the wall by humbly and desperately crying out for God's help, we quickly sense His love rushing through the opening. God will intervene where He is invited — God won't intrude where He isn't wanted.

Without God's never-ending love, we alcoholics and addicts would die trapped within our own walls. But, through the Twelve Steps of Alcoholics Anonymous, God gives us a way to discover our protective boundaries that block His attempt to rescue and restore us. These important action Steps are God helping us to realize that what we had thought was our protection is really a prison and giving us a way to free ourselves if we are ready. By working these Steps, we willingly begin to participate actively with God in the demolition of our boundaries. Through the Twelve Steps we invite and gladly permit God to crush our boundaries so that nothing stands between ourselves and His love for us.

Before the demolition job is even half finished we are amazed — amazed by God, amazed by God's extravagance. This is promised to us in the Big Book.

Are these promises extravagant? Absolutely!

Yet, they are absolutely real.

If God is willing to offer us boundless love, we must be willing to respond to Him with boundless faith in this love.

But what is boundless faith?

It goes way beyond the boundaries of human reason. Boundless faith has no stopping point. It's actually our own human extravagance in response to God's divine extravagance. Boundless faith in God's miracles is never to stop believing in the God who never stops loving. It's believing in and trusting our Creator who loves us extravagantly. Having boundless faith is simply being wide open to God's love, putting up no obstacles, and letting God love us as extravagantly as He wants to.

The Rosary as a Devotion

> *If we belong to a religious denomination which requires a definite morning devotion, we attend to that also. If not members of religious bodies, we sometimes select and memorize a few set prayers which emphasize the principles we have been discussing.*
>
> (ALCOHOLICS ANONYMOUS, p. 87)

> *It is to be hoped that every A.A. who has a religious connection which emphasizes meditation will return to the practice of that devotion as never before.*
>
> (TWELVE STEPS AND TWELVE TRADITIONS, p. 98)

OUR A.A. LITERATURE strongly suggests the return to and use of religious devotions as a spiritual tool to assist us as we try each day to come closer to God and build our relationship with him through prayer and meditation at Step Eleven.

The devotion of the rosary, a Christian daily devotion featured here in this booklet of meditations, is merely one of the many helpful devotional tools that both the Big Book and the 12&12 encourage us to put to good use on our twelve-step spiritual journey toward God as we understand God. Why do they stress the use of devotions? The obvious reason is that early A.A. members found that these things do work; almost any kind of devotion helps us to do something we aren't used to doing — meditate. Nearly all of the world's religions, and most of the denominations of Christianity, have a good variety of these wonderful spiritual aids available to help us begin to do this. It is only a matter of finding the particular one that is just right for us. I encourage you, the reader, to extend your search and be open to everything the whole religious world has to give to us who are only beginners at meditation.

Here on these pages I will introduce, present, and offer the devotion of the rosary to you as merely one devotion among many available — as one effective tool among many good effective tools.

I offer it to you simply because I have found it to work for me. Its daily use has deepened my own prayer life; it has changed my attitude of prayer; it has changed the way I openly converse with God. It has helped me to pray when praying comes hard. It has helped me to listen when listening comes hard. The rosary has taken me quickly through frustrating periods of "spiritual dryness" which could have lasted a much longer time. And further, it seems to help me see my human need to depend upon God in even the smallest things I do each day. The rosary has helped to make many changes within me. It may help you in the same way, perhaps even more so. Once again, I urge you to be open to all things and to find whatever devotion works best for you as you journey closer toward God through A.A.'s Step Eleven.

Most of us alcoholics and addicts are beginners at meditation, and we usually find it to be the most difficult aspect of Step Eleven. At least I've found it to be so. The rosary can be helpful for beginners at meditation, because it is one of the most basic and rudimentary forms of meditation. Children begin praying this devotion at a very young age, so it certainly isn't complicated. In fact, its simplicity is its beauty and its strength, for people continue to use it well into their golden years.

The Origin of the Rosary

THE DEVOTION OF THE ROSARY weaves together prayer and meditation, and its origins actually reach back to the Desert Fathers — the ancient monastic religious orders of the early fourth century. Through the ages, it has evolved and grown into the devotion that is familiar to most people today. The formation of the rosary as we know it took place in the abbeys of ninth century Ireland, and its foundation lies in the 150 Psalms of David from the Hebrew Scriptures. Thus the complete rosary consists of 150 beads, with each bead signifying one of the 150 Psalms.

The monastic practice of daily recitation of and meditation upon the Psalms (the "Divine Office") was a devotion that the laity wanted to be able to use for themselves. Illiteracy, however, was a great stumbling block for the common people of that time. Most ordinary folks could not read and thus could not be expected to master the Psalter. Later the practice of using 150 Hail Marys arose, and gradually the insertion of an Our Father before and a Glory be after each decade of Hail Marys. The insertion of "Mysteries" from New Testament salvation history developed in the fifteenth century.

This has been only a brief account, but it basically explains how the rosary, as we know and use it today, originated and has evolved. Derived from ancient monastic prayer and contemplation, it has always been the common devotion of the laity because it was born out of people's desire to experience God more intimately. And it still does today precisely what it was intended to do hundreds of years ago: it helps the ordinary person not merely to talk to God, but to begin truly to focus our attention on God and listen to Him speak to our hearts. This is meditation; and meditation is the whole purpose and function of the rosary. It is prayer and meditation upon the entire life, death and resurrection of Christ — the ultimate divine/ human encounter.

As we meditate upon the life of Jesus, the rosary simply allows us to quiet down inside, to put aside our own self-centered thoughts and begin to listen with the heart: to open the inner self to God and experience our own personal encounter with the divine.

Understanding this, it becomes clear that this devotion is dynamic, not static. It is a vehicle built and designed to bring us from one point to another, much as a bicycle is built to take us from here to there on a roadway. In the meditation of the rosary we begin at a particular place, and the rosary guides and moves us along a designated meditation path toward a new spiritual place.

This is why I like to make the bold declaration that it is impossible to pray this devotion, meditating upon Christ every day for six months, without being changed inside by it, just as it is impossible to get on a bicycle and pedal it for any distance without finding yourself at a different place from where you were before.

Meditation upon God, in this way, moves us toward God. To go toward God is to encounter God. To encounter God is to be spiritually transformed by God in the midst of this divine/human encounter.

The Role of Mary in the Rosary

ANY EXPLANATION OF THE ROSARY would be incomplete without discussing the role of Mary, the mother of Jesus, in connection with this devotion. Anyone using the rosary for the first time would certainly wonder why the prayer called the "Hail Mary" is such a prominent part of it. Why this particular prayer and not another?

I feel it necessary, then, to speak briefly about Mary and to describe the commonly-held view of her in an attempt to give reasonable answers to reasonable questions.

The earliest prayer of the rosary is the "Our Father" or the Lord's Prayer which is taken from Scripture (Matthew 6:9-13). It is also considered to be the principal prayer of this devotion. The Hail Mary actually came into use later on.

The familiar prayer called the Angelic Salutation or Hail Mary is biblically based, and its opening words can be found in the first chapter of the Gospel of St. Luke. These words are of great importance to Christianity for many reasons, but for one in particular:

The God-inspired words of Elizabeth as she paid homage to Mary (Luke 1:43) proclaim that the child that Mary carried in her womb was God Himself who had become flesh:

"Most blessed are you among women, and blessed is

the fruit of your womb. Who am I that the mother of my Lord should come to me?"

That Jesus was fully God who became fully human is the most important and basic tenet of Christianity. By echoing Elizabeth's words in homage to Mary today and also addressing her as "Holy Mary, mother of God," we ourselves fully acknowledge who Jesus is: that he is truly God. This prayer gives complete worship and glory to God; in fact, one cannot pray the Hail Mary without glorifying God. In Luke's Gospel, we see that God fully revealed Himself to Elizabeth through Mary, and Christians believe that God has never stopped using Mary to reveal Himself to humankind.

Because it is an ongoing task they believe that she still knocks at the door of the human heart seeking to bear her Son within; that she is not passively sitting up in heaven in Celestial Retirement, but actively fulfilling her never-ending God-given role of bringing Christ to all people on earth.

Christians commonly give Mary a proper place of high honor, respect, esteem, and love as the mother of God, because Scripture proclaims that God Himself bestows these blessings and graces upon her. The Hail Mary is Christianity's human response to God's view of Mary: she is highly favored in God's eyes, and therefore she is highly favored in our own. And to be sure, it was God Himself, speaking through the angel Gabriel, who first uttered the words, "Hail Mary, full of grace...."

The mother of Jesus is viewed as a spiritual mother who cares and is concerned with all of us, and so we end this prayer by asking her to intercede faithfully in prayer for us, as we would ask any family member to pray for us.

But, as we conclude this prayer by saying, "Holy Mary, Mother of God, pray for us sinners now and at the hour of our death," we are actually doing far more than merely asking for Mary's intercession. For it is here that we acknowledge something important about ourselves: that we are human beings with defects of character. In admitting this about ourselves, we acknowledge that we need the prayers of the faithful, and we acknowledge that we are in complete need of God. Here is where we can begin to arrive at the kind of humility that we seek through A.A.'s Step Seven.

Mary is never regarded as a "goddess" of any sort; nor is she adored or worshiped as one — in fact, she doesn't want to be. Mary's focus is on God alone — her "soul magnifies the Lord" (see Luke 1:46). Here's a simple example of what I mean:

Anyone can normally see a butterfly with the naked eye. Yet when we look at a butterfly through a magnifying glass, the glass always gives us a closer view and reveals the butterfly to us in a way in which we weren't able to see it before. As we look through the glass, we are always astonished to see the beauty that had previously escaped us. The glass isn't our point of focus — the butterfly is; we merely look through the glass to see the object it is focused on.

Mary focuses on God. Mary is not our point of focus; we merely look through her in order better to view the object of her focus — God. Through the prayer and meditation of the rosary we look through the faith-filled eyes of

Mary to reveal Jesus to us in a way in which we could not see him before; we allow her to "magnify the Lord," in a spiritual way, inside ourselves. Mary enables us to see more closely the infinite beauty and glory of God which has, for the most part, always escaped us. Moreover, the rosary is joining our adoration, love, faith, and prayers to God with those of Mary.

Mary plays a specific role in this devotion simply because she plays a specific God-given role in our ultimate divine/human encounter — the Incarnation of Christ. Nothing more, nothing less.

These are only a few of the basic reasons why Mary holds the place she does in Christian spirituality, in the devotion of the rosary, and in the hearts of people. But the reason for all of these is that she holds a special place in the heart of God Himself.

There is much more that could be said about Mary, but I have attempted only to give a brief but proper Christian view of her. I personally like to think of the mother of Jesus as my special "concerned-person." I have given her the honored role of mother in my recovery and in my whole life because I feel her gently guiding me toward God. This is how I personally experience her. No matter how you relate to Mary, you can still use and benefit from prayer and meditation on the rosary.

The Role of the Rosary Beads

THE OLD ENGLISH WORD FOR "PRAYER" was pronounced "bede," later spelled "bead." The physical structure of a rosary is that it is many prayers or "bedes" linked together on a chain and said in succession. Now, if one is not familiar with this devotion, it may seem at first that the purpose of rosary beads is to allow us to keep track of how many prayers we've said. But this is not so. There is no spiritual benefit to keeping track of our prayers.

Rather than helping us to keep track of prayers, the rosary beads actually allow us to lose track of time. The rosary takes about thirty minutes of our time, and for that period of meditation we can let go of time for a while and just be with God. In other words, the beads can free us from slavery to the clock in our morning meditation. If we can lose track of time for just those minutes, we can focus our whole selves — mind, body, and spirit — upon God alone, and free ourselves to listen. Listening is the only difference between delivering a monologue to God and having a dialogue with Him.

Even though my wife and I have now been married for fourteen years, I can still recall that once we began courting, getting to know each other and falling in love, time lost its significance. We had been together many times, but we began to be completely "with" each other in such a way that time stopped when we were together. We lost track of time and were always late. We didn't care. It wasn't important. Only being with each other and talking together was important. When we lost track of time, we found the freedom to focus on each other, to get to know each other in an intimate way that would have been impossible otherwise. We lost track of the hours, yet we gained a growing relationship (and a growing family with two noisy children). Gaining a growing relationship with God is the essence of Step Eleven.

It is possible to lose the importance of time in our relationship with God, in the same way my wife and I lost it in our human relationship but found the freedom to experience something else more important. Losing track of time is finding the freedom to hear God speak, to have two-way dialogue, to get to know God; freedom to build an intimate relationship with God that is otherwise nearly impossible to build. The beads are merely a tool to help us to find this freedom to be completely "with" and experience God.

The Role of Repetition: The Rhythm of The Rosary

THE PRAYERS OF THE ROSARY are rhythmic and repetitive which actually facilitates meditation. Many of us, who aren't used to this kind of prayer, would at first be hard pressed to see how repeating prayers could possibly facilitate anything. I fully understand because I once had the same feelings myself.

What happened with me was the same thing that happened when I finally worked the Twelve Steps: The Steps didn't make sense to me either. In fact they were contrary to all my first notions and inclinations. But when I ceased trying to make *sense* out of them, and began to try to make *use* of them, they became meaningful to me. The same thing happened with repetitive prayer.

Contrary to our first notions about prayer, we eventually learn that rhythmic, repetitious prayer actually opens up something inside us which was previously blocked.

In his writings, Bill W. explains that spiritual idea, and he refers to this as a "channel" being opened. In the following excerpts taken from *As Bill Sees It*, A.A.'s co-founder offers his experience on the effectiveness of this kind of prayer:

"Clearing A Channel"

During the day, we can pause where situations must be met and decisions made, and renew the simple request "Thy will, not mine, be done."

If at these points our emotional disturbance happens to be great, we will more surely keep our balance provided we remember, and repeat to ourselves, a particular prayer or phrase that has appealed to us in our reading or meditation. Just saying it over and over will often enable us to clear a channel choked up with anger, fear, frustration, or misunderstanding, and permit us to return to the surest help of all — our search for God's will, not our own, in the moment of stress. (As Bill Sees It, p. 78)

"Prayer Under Pressure"

Whenever I find myself under acute tensions, I lengthen my daily walks and slowly repeat our Serenity Prayer in rhythm to my steps and breathing.

If I feel that my pain has in part been occasioned by others, I try to repeat, "God, grant me the serenity to love their best, and never fear their worst." This benign healing process of repetition, sometimes necessary to persist with for days, has seldom failed to restore me to at least a workable emotional balance and perspective. (As Bill Sees It, p. 250)

Out of his own experience at prayer, Bill speaks of moving from inner conflict to inner peace by using simple repetitive prayer. In the midst of extreme fear and anger, it enabled him to get reconnected with God, who changed his perception of things and restored his sanity and serenity.

If this type of prayer can have that kind of positive impact on our spirit in the midst of stormy emotions, it makes sense that it would be even more effective as we begin our day. However we're still left with the big question WHY? Why does it "enable us to clear a channel"? Why does it "permit us to return to the surest help of all"? When we consider it more fully, its practicality becomes a little clearer.

When we observe nature, we see that everything in God's good creation has a natural, repetitive, rhythmic flow, from the sea tides to the cycles of the four seasons, from the revolution of the earth around the sun to the repetitive cycles of birth, life and death of all living things in creation. All of life constantly repeats itself over and over at God's command. We know that birds fly, fish swim, people walk, and the human heart beats by rhythmic, repetitive motion as God intended. Life is not static — it moves repeatedly. Rhythmic repetition is the most natural thing in life. Through this devotion, we can let ourselves be soothed by the rosary's natural, rhythmic flow and come to sense a positive spiritual, mental and physical connectedness with the God who created the very rhythms of life. This human connectedness with our Divine God is where that "healing process," which Bill speaks of, begins.

Potholes and Bumps Along the Way

IN DISCUSSING PRAYER AND MEDITATION, it always helps me when some attention is given to the troubling things that can trip us up and hinder our spiritual progress. The difficulties they can cause are real and I've stumbled into some of these "spiritual potholes" myself. God is making the way straight for us but we can place stumbling blocks in our way by our distorted ways of thinking. So a safe journey means that we will need to change some of the ways we think about prayer, meditation, ourselves and God. The pitfalls I've experienced all seem to have these common denominators:

- They always contain the word "enough."
- They mainly consist of a distorted idea of "measuring."
- They all lead me to believe that I don't measure up.
- They always bring me to the hopeless conclusion that there is no point in continuing further.
- They are all utterly false.

A car being driven down a road can develop various kinds of car troubles, yet no matter what type of trouble arises, it always does the same thing; it brings the car to a stop on the road. The path we've now come to walk is, by its nature, a path of faith. Faith in God is the very thing that is driving us down the road. On a faith-path all sorts of troubles can develop, but they all really do the same thing; they cause doubt, and doubt always brings us to a grinding halt on the path. Every difficulty we have along the way, no matter what kind we think it is, is always based on doubt — doubts about ourselves, about God, about everything.

The first among these troubles is one I call the Emotional-Feelings-Trap; the self-defeating notion that meditation should emotionally affect us, or give us a certain kind of good feeling, or produce a glorious sensation, if we are "doing it well enough." The truth is that emotions are such a fickle thing that they are totally unreliable as a measuring device for how we are doing at meditation.

The daily practice of meditation has its effects, but they are never the ones we expect. Some of the consequences of meditation that we're likely to see are those which manifest themselves in our everyday affairs when we are not even meditating. We may, for no apparent reason, feel like forgiving an insult; or contrary to our best interests, feel like helping a person; or begin to feel compassion for someone; or even react to negative events in more positive ways than we did before.

Sometimes we actually do feel strong feelings of happiness, or gratitude, or consolation, or joy during meditation itself; sometimes we don't. But, if we don't, it never means we aren't doing it right. If we use momentary feelings as a measuring stick for meditation, we're certain to come up short.

Distractions are the next pitfall that can trouble us. Anyone who seriously tries meditation knows that human beings have minds that tend to wander. But the mind never wanders aimlessly — it always drifts back toward the Self. No matter how determined we are to raise our minds and hearts toward God for care and direction, most of us find that something inside us seems to direct our attention away from God and back toward our own preoccupations.

I don't know anyone, in or out of A.A., who doesn't feel a bit frustrated when they see this happening. But, some of us in recovery make federal cases out of the smallest matters. The worst hazard is that we can then begin to feel badly about ourselves, and how we think God feels about us. Thoughts like this are guaranteed to surface when we make meditation a pass/fail situation. The whole thing becomes a deadly trap, because we can never clearly define what "passing" means — therefore, we're doomed to "fail."

The important thing to remember is that the only way it is possible to actually fail at meditation is to *not* do it. We can win by simply showing up.

Acknowledging our need for God is the surest way to break an opening through which we can enter into meditation. We simply begin by surrendering to God that we are human, with human weaknesses and limitations. God understands and allows for our limitations — it is we who often won't allow ourselves to be what God made us to be.

It was in my surrender to my own humanity that God helped me to accept His love for my humanness by reminding me of the fact that I am a father myself; the father of a daughter who loves to draw pictures. He then used this very fact to show me how He sees me.

Think of a little girl drawing a picture with crayons,

and presenting it to her daddy. Artistically speaking, it's crudely-made and very imperfect, but the father is elated, nonetheless. He doesn't reject his child's gift because of its flaws; he lovingly accepts it merely because of who it came from. Even though she has colored outside the lines and failed to make it perfectly, it's a treasure in his eyes because he treasures his child.

God treasures us, too.

He is our Father, we are His children. God will always accept our smallest gifts, no matter how many times we've colored outside the lines, no matter how many mistakes we think we've made, no matter how crudely-made our gifts are. God is absolutely elated just because it is His own children who have brought the gifts. He loves us, and treasures each one of our imperfect attempts to bring ourselves to Him in meditation. So, don't be overly concerned with "staying inside the lines" or doing it perfectly — just make all your attempts at meditation as best you can, and bring them to God, knowing they will be accepted with love. Remember, if the child drew pictures for her dad, but threw them away because they didn't seem good enough to give him, the child and her father would've both failed to experience the moment of sharing them together. At Step Eleven, we'd probably like to be able to meditate like saints, yet we'd be much better off to come to Him like little children. In truth, this is the way most of the saints really came to God — as children. The following true story shows how God used my daughter, Katie, to make His point clear.

For several weeks I'd been having that old feeling that I was nothing but a spiritual wasteland, and my prayer time was such an empty exercise that I hadn't been feeling like praying at all. Nevertheless, I still got up early to "do the drill," along with praying the rosary each morning. Then one Saturday afternoon, Katie and I were driving to the grocery store in my old pick-up truck. She was chattering on about the kinds of things that normal eight-year-olds think about, when her childlike banter was momentarily interrupted, like a radio station breaks from its format for a short news flash. Looking at me with eyes as blue and clear as the summer sky, she calmly stated, "Dad, you don't have to be worried and afraid about any of those things. Jesus says to tell you that he's very proud of you and pleased with the way you've been praying to him."

And that was that.

Her tone was firm, yet benevolent. Her message delivered, she then returned to her childish conversation as if she hadn't said anything out of the ordinary. Katie knew nothing of my worries, doubts and fears and probably wouldn't have comprehended them anyway. I hadn't told anyone — except God. A million questions now shot through me all at once. But I could only look at her.

"If only that were true," I thought.

But, as I replayed each word in my mind again, I was struck with a certain something about HOW those words were spoken. The words had come marching out of my daughter's mouth like a hundred Roman soldiers sent into battle by the Centurion who had authority to give the order, authority given him by the General who had authority given to him by a higher authority, and so on. That was it. I knew that the words I'd just heard were spoken with....authority. Yes. Authority that reached back through every word of Holy Scripture, through the Gospels, through the Apostles and Prophets, through the Last Supper and the Crucifixion and the Resurrection, through the Torah and Moses and Abraham, from age to age to age, to the beginning of time. I'd been so busy with the words, I nearly overlooked the most important part of the message — the authority part: "Jesus says..."

I now understood.

Authority. My doubts turned-tail and fled at once. They simply could not stand up in the face of it. A new childlike security came as we rode on together, knowing that the Father is pleased with me, His child, just as I'm pleased with Katie, my child.

We can never know how or when God will say He loves us, but rest assured that any bump or pothole in the road is nothing compared to the power of His love that draws us to Him as we walk the path of faith.

The Role of Devotional Books in Meditation

*Prayer is the raising of the heart and mind to God
— and in this sense it includes meditation.*
(TWELVE STEPS AND TWELVE TRADITIONS, p. 102)

OUR WANDERING MINDS are a big reason why the use of daily devotional books, prayer books, Scripture reading, or passages from the Big Book and other A.A. literature are so important to us. It is helpful to give our minds something outside of ourselves to rest upon or focus on. And this is why I have provided this small devotional booklet: to let the readings help you to paint mental pictures and to let your mind become involved in them, yet ultimately, to let your heart become involved.

It is said that the farthest distance in the whole world is the distance between the mind and the heart. In our recovery process, our mind receives a lot of good information — but that information must cause a transformation. It must move from the mind to the heart if it is going to make a difference. And this spiritual transformation is certainly what can happen, but in order for it to happen it is necessary that we have an open heart. Meditation upon spiritual readings is an effective way gradually to become more open-hearted and vulnerable to God, to be as defenseless as a child before God, and to allow our whole selves to be transformed by God.

The rhythmic prayers of the rosary coupled with the scriptural meditations found here can allow us to open up a closed and disconnected self and to connect our whole being, mind, body, and spirit, with God. Once again, don't strive for perfection; accept that it probably won't be perfect. Simply go to God and present your imperfect gift of yourself, desiring to hear Him and to be changed and transformed as He desires.

The Traditional Rosary

AS I STATED EARLIER, the traditional rosary focuses upon the whole life of Christ: his annunciation and birth, his passion and death, his resurrection and ascension into heaven — his life in its entirety. These crucial saving acts of Jesus, called Mysteries, are meditated upon as one prays the rosary. Therefore, these meditations are traditionally known as the Joyful, the Sorrowful, and the Glorious Mysteries of the rosary. This is the format of the fifteen-decade traditional rosary used throughout the world:

The Five Joyful Mysteries:
1. The Annunciation
2. The Visitation
3. The Birth of Jesus
4. The Presentation of Jesus in the Temple
5. The Finding of Jesus in the Temple

The Five Sorrowful Mysteries:
1. The Agony of Jesus in the Garden
2. The Scourging of Jesus at the Pillar
3. The Crowning of Jesus with Thorns
4. The Carrying of the Cross
5. The Crucifixion of Jesus

The Five Glorious Mysteries:
1. The Resurrection of Jesus
2. The Ascension of Jesus into Heaven
3. The Descent of the Holy Spirit upon the Apostles
4. The Assumption of Mary into Heaven
5. The Crowning of Mary in Heaven

This form is the one I've most often used, and it has proven most effective for me. I urge you to learn it and use it if you desire.

Here is a traditional way of praying the rosary:

One may contemplate the five Joyful Mysteries on Monday, the five Sorrowful Mysteries on Tuesday, and the five Glorious Mysteries on Wednesday; beginning again with the five Joyful ones on Thursday, the Sorrowful on Friday, and the Glorious on Saturday. The Glorious Mysteries are prayed on Sunday. This is one common way. Some people will, however, often meditate upon all fifteen Mysteries in a single day. Either way is beneficial. To experience the full impact of this devotion, I encourage this traditional form. There are many devotional booklets available on the traditional rosary, which can be obtained from most religious bookstores. I urge you to search them out if you would like to learn more about this devotion.

Although these key points in Christ's life are the ones most commonly used for the rosary, other parts of scripture can also be used for meditation.

So what I would like to do in this book is to take this traditional prayer and adapt it to fit our particular needs. I call this form the Healing Rosary.

The Healing Rosary

THE ROSARY AS I PRESENT IT TO YOU HERE is slightly different from the traditional. It consists of only five mysteries to ponder instead of fifteen. It focuses upon Jesus' life as the traditional devotion does, but it concentrates on a particular part of his life: the three years before his crucifixion.

It is here that we see Jesus interacting with people — people who are just like us. We see him speaking with them One-on-one, loving them, touching them individually, changing their lives, and healing them. This is the context of his life on earth in which the ordinary people encountered Jesus — troubled people, hurting people, people with everyday living problems, the average and the below-average human beings who faced daily hardship, the ones who suffered physically and emotionally; the good, the bad, the sad, the hated, and the forgotten of society; the street people, the misfits, the throw-aways, the nobodies.

It is because of these people — desperate, hurting people who walked, limped, crawled, or were carried over many miles of dusty, rough and rocky roads to find Jesus, hoping and believing that he would drastically change their lives for the better, that I had to write these pages. It is because of them that I have written these meditations on the miracles of Jesus.

As I read about these people in Scripture and spent time meditating upon these healings, I found myself, as a recovering alcoholic, able to relate to each afflicted, suffering person.

I could sense their pain and desperation, because I had been in pain and desperation at Step One. They had "come to believe" that Jesus could restore them, and so had I at Step Two. They had decided to make their slow, painful, sometimes difficult journey toward him, and I had as well at Step Three. I understood them, and I felt that they would understand me just as easily. Passages from the Big Book began to come to my mind as I thought about these suffering people.

One of the many things that struck me about them was the extreme lengths they were willing to go to just to find Jesus, to get near him, to talk to him, to ask to be healed. They traveled hundreds of miles, they fought their way through crowds, they risked humiliation and abuse, they tore the roofs right off houses to get to wherever he was — and why?

Faith.

Pure, crazy, outrageously hopeful, absolutely unexplainable faith. Would I have had their kind of faith to go that far? Would I have risked everything that they did? Or would I have started out on the journey, only to turn back at some rough point? I wasn't sure — I'm still not. I am only sure that I didn't have their kind of faith in him at the outset of my own journey toward God. But this was the kind of faith I knew I needed in my recovery now, so I began to accompany these people on their journey toward Jesus in my morning meditations.

As I walked with them through the rosary in my daily meditations, they brought me right where they were going: to the awesome, powerful, loving presence of Jesus who heals all human brokenness. I began to see him differently. More and more I began to see Jesus not as I'd always seen him before, but as they were seeing him. More importantly, however, I began to see how Jesus saw them.

Society had seen all these people as trash to be thrown away, but Jesus had seen each one of them as a priceless, precious treasure worth saving. He had healed them because he loved and valued them, and this was what had its greatest impact on my faith.

I had taken note of the great lengths that these desperate people had gone to in order to approach Jesus, but I began to see the extreme lengths that he was willing to go to in order to heal them. In faith those people who were "unclean" had crossed a well-defined line to encounter Jesus, and he had crossed that line as well. He healed people on the sabbath, entered the homes of Gentiles and even ate dinner with them, touched lepers and allowed others who were considered "ritually unclean" to touch him. Even making the clay in his fingers to put on the blind man's eyes was an infraction of traditional rules. He breached the boundaries that separated humanity from God. Each healing encounter was humanity and God stepping across a barrier to embrace each other — human faith and divine love crossing each other's boundaries. From the divine side of these encounters, the value of a human being was the reason for healing. From the human side, faith was essential in accepting that healing.

For some, their faith had made the difference between living life again or dying the wretched death of a leper. For others, it was the difference between walking home or remaining crippled and stuck by the roadside on a beggar's pallet watching life pass them by. For me today, faith makes the difference between living a new, happy life with my family and friends or painfully drinking until I slowly died the gruesome death that only alcoholics die. Faith was the difference for them and for me, for I began to get a glimpse of how God loves and values me.

Their faith is contagious. I caught it, and you will certainly catch it too. I invite you to walk with these people. Go with the blind, the crippled, the lepers, and the other misfits and outcasts of society. You'll find all their stories in your own Bible. As you read them, travel by their side as they approach and encounter Jesus of Nazareth.

I invite you to approach and encounter Jesus in these five rosary meditations and catch a glimpse of his endless love for you. Cross the "line." Go to him. Bring him your own brokenness, your own suffering. Approach him humbly and ask him to heal you, just as these people of long ago did.

As you go, keep this firmly fixed in your mind: not one single afflicted person was ever turned down and sent away.

How to Use the Rosary

THE ROSARY ALWAYS BEGINS on the crucifix. Traditionally, the first prayer of this devotion is the Apostle's Creed. This prayer is a universal statement of Christian faith. This may, however, not be your particular statement of Christian faith. If you wish, you can begin simply by praying the Third Step and the Seventh Step Prayers together as one universal prayer, for these two A.A. prayers, said as one, are truly the alcoholic's universal prayer asking our Creator to heal us. It is certainly our worldwide statement of faith.

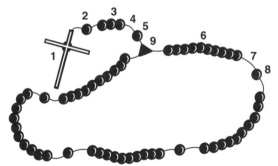

1. To begin, on the crucifix:

Pray the Third and Seventh Step Prayers:

God, I offer myself to Thee — to build with me and to do with me as Thou wilt. Relieve me of the bondage of self, that I may better do Thy will. Take away my difficulties, that victory over them may bear witness to those I would help of Thy Power, Thy Love, and Thy Way of life. May I do Thy will always.

My Creator, I am now willing that you should have all of me, good and bad. I pray that you now remove from me every single defect of character which stands in the way of my usefulness to you and my fellows. Grant me strength, as I go out from here to do your bidding. Amen.

2. On the first single bead:

Pray the Our Father:

Our Father who art in Heaven, hallowed be Thy name. Thy Kingdom come, Thy will be done on earth as it is in heaven. Give us this day our daily bread, and forgive us our trespasses, as we forgive those who trespass against us. And lead us not into temptation, but deliver us from evil. *For Thine is the Kingdom, and the Power, and the Glory forever and ever. Amen.*

(Note: While this doxology is not included in the actual words of Jesus' prayer of Matthew 6:9-13, it is a common way of ending the Lord's Prayer at most A.A. meetings.)

3. On each one of the next three beads:

Pray the Hail Mary:

Hail Mary full of grace, the Lord is with thee. Blessed art thou among women and blessed is the fruit of thy womb, Jesus. Holy Mary, mother of God, pray for us sinners now and at the hour of our death. Amen.

4. On the space after the three beads:

Pray the Glory be to the Father:

Glory be to the Father, and to the Son, and to the Holy Spirit as it was in the beginning, is now and ever shall be, world without end. Amen.

At this point, announce the First Healing Mystery and read the first Scripture reading. While meditating upon the reading, pray the Our Father on the next single bead (**5**), and one Hail Mary upon each one of the following ten beads (**6**). Each set of ten beads on the rosary is called a "decade."

End this set of ten beads, or decade, by praying the Glory be to the Father on the space that follows (**7**).

When finished, move on to the next single bead (**8**) and announce the Second Healing Mystery. Repeat this process of announcing each Healing Mystery, praying one Our Father, ten Hail Marys, and one Glory be, while meditating on each mystery. Continue until all five Healing Mysteries have been completed. Thus for each Mystery you pray one Our Father, ten Hail Marys, and one Glory be.

9. To end the rosary:

The final prayer of the rosary is called the "Hail Holy Queen." This prayer is recited at the end of the Fifth Healing Mystery.

"Hail, holy Queen, mother of mercy, our life, our sweetness and our hope. To you do we cry, poor banished children of Eve; to you do we send up our sighs, mourning and weeping in this valley of tears. Turn, then, most gracious advocate, your eyes of compassion toward us, and after this our exile, show unto us the blessed fruit of your womb, Jesus. O clement, O loving, O sweet Virgin Mary!"

This brief response may be prayed at the end. "Pray for us, O holy mother of God, that we may be made worthy of the promises of Christ."

Many of the miracles of Jesus, which the Gospels tell us about, were healings of the physical body. The Gospels also demonstrate that other people needed the kind of healing that wasn't physical; some needed healing of the mind, and some needed healing of the spirit. And we see that Jesus responded to these kinds of human needs by miraculously restoring them back to good mental or spiritual health.

But Jesus did not limit his miracles to the healing of physical, mental, or spiritual conditions. A good number of his miracles were actually the healing, or the restoration of conditions, situations, or circumstances of life — the human problems of everyday living.

The Gospels show us that Christ performed all kinds of miracles for all kinds of people with all kinds of needs; that his miracles always met a human need in some way. Whether it was a lack of physical health, a lack of wine at a wedding reception, a lack of food for a famished crowd, or the lack of calm seas to travel, Jesus' miracles always restored whatever was lacking in the situation.

Therefore the miracles I have chosen for meditation here in the following five healing mysteries are healings of various kinds. We will see Jesus healing human beings, and we'll see him healing their human situations as well. Pondering all these different types of miracles has helped me to increasingly trust him with different aspects of my own life, knowing he will miraculously meet every kind of human need I may have; healing and restoring whatever is broken or lacking in my life.

The First Healing Mystery

THE WEDDING FEAST AT CANA

John 2:1-11

...There was a wedding in Cana in Galilee, and the mother of Jesus was there. Jesus and his disciples were also invited to the wedding. When the wine ran short, the mother of Jesus said to him, "They have no wine." Jesus said to her, "Woman, how does your concern affect me? My hour has not yet come." His mother said to the servers, "Do whatever he tells you." Now there were six stone water jars there for ceremonial washings, each holding twenty to thirty gallons. Jesus told them, "Fill the jars with water." So they filled them to the brim. Then he told them, "Draw some out now, and take it to the headwaiter." So they took it. And when the headwaiter tasted the water that had become wine, without knowing where it came from (although the servers who had drawn the water knew), the headwaiter called the bridegroom and said to him, "Everyone serves good wine first, and then when people have drunk freely, an inferior one; but you have kept the good wine until now." Jesus did this as the beginning of his signs in Cana in Galilee and so revealed his glory, and his disciples began to believe in him.

Reflection

As they stood before Jesus listening to his instructions to fill all the water jars, the servants at Cana must have had a number of questions racing through their minds, and the first one was probably this:

"How could plain water be any kind of solution to a wine problem?"

They understood his instructions all right — they couldn't have understood his solution. Nevertheless, because they understood that they were servants, they listened unquestioningly as Jesus placed their simple task before them.

Now, what Jesus was asking them to do was nothing new or difficult for them. As servants, they had gone outside to the well and filled those water jars and brought them in every day for their master. Jesus wasn't asking them to do anything radical.

But only moments before, the determined woman who had sent them to him had suggested something to them that was totally radical.

"Do whatever he tells you," she had said — and she pointed to Jesus.

What was so radical?

Jesus was nobody to them. He was just another wedding guest. He was not their master. They already had a master whom they obediently served. They were working only under his orders to bring food and drink to his invited guests. They did only whatever he told them. These men certainly didn't take orders from Jesus. But here was a guest, (a woman no less) telling them to go to Jesus and treat him as their master, to listen to him as a servant listens only to his master, to obey him as a servant obeys his master — to do whatever he tells them. That was different.

That was radical.

Yet, the dilemma at Cana called for radical action. Mary knew that their regular master had no power to change this situation — no matter how many gallons of water they brought him. But Mary knew in faith that if they went to her Son and followed his orders, Jesus would provide what was needed.

Mary's faith was radical, and her words were radical, but what followed at this wedding reception at Cana was even more radical.

> *This is the how and the why of it. First of all, we had to quit playing God. It didn't work. Next, we decided that hereafter in this drama of life, God was going to be our Director. He is the Principal; we are His agents. He is the Father, and we are His children. Most good ideas are simple, and this concept was the keystone of the new and triumphant arch through which we passed to freedom. When we sincerely took such a position, all sorts of remarkable things followed. We had a new Employer. Being all powerful, He provided what we needed if we kept close to Him and performed His work well.*

(ALCOHOLICS ANONYMOUS, pp. 62-63)

This is Step Three. Radical? You bet.

But because of the hopelessness of our own dilemma, this is Alcoholics Anonymous' radical call to "do whatever he tells you."

It's changing the master we serve.

As we work through Step Three we begin to invite God more and more into our lives and things start to get a little better. But when we find ourselves lacking the faith to meet the occasional difficulties of living sober, our sponsors point out to us that we need to make a radical change. They tell us that we've invited God into our lives — but as only a house guest. He's there, and we're glad He's there, but we're still the master of the house. We are still the master of our own life, our own will — the master of our self. Then our sponsors help us to realize that the master whom we've always obediently served has no power to change anything in our lives.

As Mary did at Cana, they radically suggest that we change the master we serve and they point us to God.

Our sponsors then comfort us by showing us that it is never God who asks us to do things that are out of our reach or beyond our human capabilities — it is ourselves, as masters of our own lives, who always put humanly impossible tasks before us.

We can never understand God's solutions to our human dilemmas. Yet our sponsors urge us, as Mary did at Cana, simply to try to "do whatever" He puts in front of us, and we'll see amazing results. In Alcoholics Anonymous, just as at Cana, we find the Step Three suggestion to be totally radical. But we also find that the work of the Program is well within our human reach. And the results

— sobriety, sanity, and serenity — are absolutely miraculous.

Meditation

Our hearts can only hear the voice of the master we serve. If it is myself I serve, I can only hear my own voice. If it is God, I will hear His voice with clarity. As I begin this day, I stand listening as a servant listens, ready to do the work of my master.

While meditating upon the reading, pray:

One Our Father
Ten Hail Marys
One Glory be to the Father

The Second Healing Mystery

THE HEALING OF A MAN BORN BLIND

John 9:1-3, 6-9

As [Jesus] passed by he saw a man blind from birth. His disciples asked him, "Rabbi, who sinned, this man or his parents, that he was born blind?" Jesus answered them, "Neither he nor his parents sinned; it is so that the works of God might be made visible through him."...[Then Jesus] spat on the ground and made clay with the saliva, and smeared the clay on his eyes, and said to him, "Go wash in the Pool of Siloam."...So he went and washed, and came back able to see.

His neighbors and those who had seen him earlier as a beggar said, "Isn't this the one who used to sit and beg?" Some said, "It is," but others said, "No, he just looks like him." He said, "I am [the one]."

Reflection

In Jesus' time, many people believed one thing about chronic, incurable illness: If you had it, God had apparently had it with you. Blindness from birth, it was assumed, must surely be a just punishment from an angry God for sins committed by yourself or even by someone else in your family long ago deceased. God, as they understood him, handed out suffering to bad people. God was very unapproachable and had a long memory.

As they looked closely at the blind man, the disciples couldn't really see any bad in him, and they were puzzled by this. That's why they asked Jesus the question: "Who sinned...?" Yet, they still clung to the old idea that he, or somebody of his clan, must be pretty bad. Jesus knew they felt this way. But, worse than this, he knew that this unfortunate blind man must certainly feel the same way too: that since he was born blind, he must be just plain bad and God must be extremely angry with him. The disciples had looked at the man to see the bad in him. But when Jesus looked at him, he saw not a bad man — he saw only a broken man.

This stopped Jesus in his tracks. Wherever he had to go, whatever he had to do, it wasn't all that important now — this man was important to him now. This destructive thinking only drove suffering people away from God, not toward Him. This idea had to go. So, right now, it was time for "show and tell."

When the blind beggar was brought to his attention, Jesus seized this perfect opportunity to show God's love and mercy for all people by healing this man right where everyone could see it happen. He had been telling them many things about the love of the Father but, right then, by his healing actions, he showed them a God very different from what they had ever understood before. Jesus showed everyone a God who doesn't angrily seek to punish bad people, but a God who lovingly wants to heal broken people.

Through the miracles of Jesus, people came to see God as He really is. And through those healing wonders many broken, cast-off, suffering people became able to approach the "unapproachable God."

The merciful works of God were truly made visible to them all that day. As the blind man washed his eyes and came back to the people with his sight restored, their conception of an angry, punishing God was washed away in the pool right along with his blindness.

Today we alcoholics and addicts often see God much as these people did two thousand years ago: angry, vengeful, and ready to punish us for our shortcomings. To those of us who feel that we are bad, God seems very unapproachable too.

But as we see the many miracles in Alcoholics Anonymous, our doubts and fears about God are washed away by His healing actions in the lives of the people we see Him touch. And we come to believe that we can approach God too. Like those who saw this miracle happen two thousand years ago, we get to see God as He really is — eager to love us, ready to forgive us, and willing to heal us.

They had seen miracles, and one was to come to them. They had visioned the Great Reality — their loving and All Powerful Creator.

(ALCOHOLICS ANONYMOUS, p. 161)

Like the street beggar who was given new sight, many people who knew us before do not recognize us today either. But as we live new, productive, sober lives and tell our stories around the tables, we assure them: "I am the one."

Meditation

Is my conception of God based upon how I would play God? Whenever I play God, I am always a God of justice, never a God of mercy. It is always me who unmercifully punishes me for my wrongs — not God. Today I will let God be the God of love and mercy that he really is. Today I will let Him touch me and heal my brokenness.

While meditating upon the reading, pray:

One Our Father
Ten Hail Marys
One Glory be to the Father

The Third Healing Mystery

PETER WALKS ON WATER

Matthew 14:22-33

[After feeding about five thousand men and their families a large meal of bread and fish, Jesus] made the disciples get into the boat and precede him to the other side, while . . . he went up on the mountain by himself to pray. When it was evening he was there alone. Meanwhile the boat, already a few miles off shore, was being tossed about by the waves, for the wind was against it. During the fourth watch of the night,* he came toward them, walking on the sea. When the disciples saw him walking on the sea they were terrified. "It is a ghost," they said, and they cried out in fear. At once [Jesus] spoke to them, "Take courage, it is I; do not be afraid." Peter said to him in reply, "Lord, if it is you, command me to come to you on the water." He said, "Come." Peter got out of the boat and began to walk on the water toward Jesus. But, when he saw how [strong] the wind was he became frightened and, beginning to sink, he cried out, "Lord, save me!" Immediately Jesus stretched out his hand and caught him, and said to him, "O you of little faith, why did you doubt?" After they got into the boat, the wind died down. Those who were in the boat did him homage, saying, "Truly, you are the Son of God."

*some time between 3:00 a.m. and 6:00 a.m.

Reflection

With a courageous faith in who really was walking on the water out there in the dark, Peter boldly stepped out of a perfectly good boat onto the rough and unpredictable sea of Galilee — fully believing that, because of Jesus' power and authority over all of nature, the water would now hold him up, if Jesus commanded Peter to come walking to him.

Well, it did. Now, the other men in the boat were probably pretty shocked when they saw the water holding Peter up. Peter surely wasn't very surprised at all. Even to consider getting out of the boat, he obviously had loads of faith in Jesus' power.

But Peter must have been quite surprised to learn how quickly the whole scene could change in his mind; and he must have been pretty disappointed in himself that he didn't do his walk of faith perfectly. Peter must have wondered what had happened.

Jesus saw the great faith that was steadily growing in the courageous heart of this rugged Galilean fisherman and, when he pulled him back up on top of the water again, he helped him to understand what had happened: that it wasn't really the strength of the winds and the roughness of the seas that had sunk him — it was something else that had brought him down.

In just a few words, Jesus explained to Peter that, as he climbed out of the boat and walked with his full attention directed on Jesus, he had walked on water relying totally on "Jesus Power." But as soon as he began to direct his attention to the adverse conditions around him instead of to Jesus, and began to struggle against the winds — he began to rely on "Peter power." This is when Peter started to doubt Jesus and began to trust himself. God's will had kept him on top; self-will had almost put him under.

When Peter forgot that Jesus was really there with him and began to see himself as just a man standing there all alone out on the water — just him, the rolling waves, the deep dark sea, and the fierce winds — gut-wrenching fear began to grip him.

> *We reviewed our fears thoroughly. We put them on paper, even though we had no resentment in connection with them. We asked ourselves why we had them. Wasn't it because self-reliance failed us? Self-reliance was good as far as it went, but it didn't go far enough. The verdict of the ages is that faith means courage. All men of faith have courage. They trust their God.* (ALCOHOLICS ANONYMOUS, p. 68)

A.A.'s Step Four inventory is God's command to "come"; to climb out of where we are and trust that because God is with us, we can fearlessly step out and walk in sobriety. Step Four takes no less courage for us than walking on water did for Peter. Yet those A.A.s who have walked before us assure us that we can trust and rely upon the power of God's command.

But just as Peter was still learning, so are we still learning how to walk in complete faith that God is always there with us, that by His power we can live sober no matter how hard the "wind is blowing" in our lives. Peter fell short on his walk of faith, but falling short is a very human thing to do. Sometimes we just don't do it perfectly, no matter how long we've been clean and sober or how much faith we have.

But out there on top of the water, Jesus knew how human Peter really was and, when he called out asking for help, Jesus immediately saved him — even though Peter didn't do it perfectly.

> *We ask Him to remove our fear and direct our attention to what He would have us be. At once, we commence to outgrow fear.* (ALCOHOLICS ANON., p. 68)

Walking on water certainly seems humanly impossible to do. But is it? For us alcoholics and addicts, living clean and sober is just as impossible and just as miraculous. When we look at ourselves to see that, by God's power, we are now holding jobs, accepting responsibilities, caring about others, helping people, mending hopelessly damaged relationships, and walking unnoticed among normal people in society, what miracle is bigger than this?

Compared to these wonders, what's a little stroll across water?

Meditation

No matter how many times I lose faith and become afraid, no matter how many times I fall short of what God would have me be — God will always reach out His hand and pull me back to my feet when I call out to Him for help.

While meditating upon the reading, pray:

One Our Father
Ten Hail Marys
One Glory be to the Father

The Fourth Healing Mystery

THE HEALING OF A LEPER

Mark 1:35-45

Rising very early before dawn, he left and went off to a deserted place, where he prayed. Simon and those who were with him pursued him and on finding him said, "Everyone is looking for you." He told them, "Let us go on to the nearby villages that I may preach there also. For this purpose have I come." So he went into their synagogues, preaching and driving out demons throughout the whole of Galilee.

A leper came to him [and kneeling down] begged him and said, "If you wish, you can make me clean. Moved with pity, he stretched out his hand, touched him, and said to him, "I do will it. Be made clean." The leprosy left him immediately, and he was made clean. Then, warning him sternly, he dismissed him at once. Then he said to him, "See that you tell no one anything, but go, show yourself to the priest and offer for your cleansing what Moses prescribed; that will be proof for them." The man went away and began to publicize the whole matter. He spread the report abroad so that it was impossible for Jesus to enter a town openly. He remained outside in deserted places, and people kept coming to him from everywhere.

Reflection

Because of the terrible destructive nature of his disease — the ghastly stench, gruesome deformity of the body, and fear of contagion — lepers like this man were driven away from populated areas, and they took their place at a distance on the outer fringes of society. The safest distance for a leper to stay from people was what we would call "hollering distance," or about a hundred yards.

As a man covered with leprosy, the poor fellow who knelt down before Jesus had taken a huge risk by walking toward him and placing himself in such a vulnerable position on his knees. Feared and despised by people, and believed to be despised and "cursed" by God, this man was used to being chased away with sticks or having stones hurled at him if he came too near a village. Common sense would tell anyone in his position to approach with caution, stay on his feet, and be ready to run if necessary. But this leper's common sense had nothing to do with his healing encounter with Jesus on this day — his hope and faith, however, had absolutely everything to do with it.

From a distance, he had intently watched as Jesus was causing quite a big stir inside the village. Crowds were gathering and he saw something that caused quite a stir inside him. Jesus was reaching out and touching people, being kind to people, and healing people. But not just ordinary people; no, these people were the scum of the earth, the untouchable ones, the unlovable ones, the incurable ones, the "cursed" ones — and he was turning none of them away.

As he stood there on the outside watching, the man came to believe that Jesus could heal him too. Whether he would or not, he didn't know — for he was an outcast even among outcasts. But he had something now that he had never had before: he now had hope. And he decided that walking toward Jesus was a risk worth taking.

It was then that all his common sense left him. For him, common sense would thus become uncommon sense, and the man began walking toward Jesus. And when he got near, he immediately fell to his knees, humbly offering himself to him. Jesus could do whatever he wanted with the man, and he told Jesus so.

As he knelt there in the dirt, he told Jesus that he believed that he could heal him if he wanted to. Mercy was a thing he was silently hoping for, yet it was something a man like him couldn't ask for.

But when Jesus moved toward him, the man felt something that someone in his position could never have dared to ask for: he felt Jesus put his hand right on him and touch him — not to hurt him but to heal him. He laid his hand directly on his disease-ravaged skin — skin so infected and ugly that no one wanted even to look at it, let alone touch it; but Jesus touched him — putrid stench, wretched open sores, decaying flesh and all. And then he heard Jesus kindly assure him that he wanted to heal him just as much as he wanted to be healed.

And there in a vulnerable position, on his knees in the dirt, he was healed of his disease.

Imagine the powerful sensation he must have felt flowing through him as his whole body was being changed, restored, and healed. Imagine his troubled mind and wounded spirit, now unburdened from guilt and shame, free to know that the very same judgmental God who, he thought, had "cursed" him, had now, reached out His loving hand to heal him.

Imagine his joy! His life was now brand new! No wonder the man couldn't contain himself. Could anyone actually keep quiet about a miracle such as this? Could I? Could you?

Feeling that we are hated and rejected by both humanity and God, we alcoholics and addicts in recovery today always begin our walk toward God from the outer fringes of life, as this leper did. Because of the horribly destructive nature of our disease, many people have chased us out of their lives in disgust too. We see ourselves as just as unclean and unlovable as this leper saw himself, and approaching God seems like risky business for us too.

Even as we come to our first few A.A. meetings, we find a safe place at the outer fringes of Alcoholics Anonymous: the chairs against the back wall, in the corner, behind the coffee pot, or by the door, so that we can be ready to run if necessary — but always on the outside. Yet, from the outer fringes of A.A. we, like the leper, can still see God in action healing people like us; and hope is stirred inside us too. As we watch God heal others, we eventually come to believe that we could take the huge risk of walking toward Him through the Twelve Steps of Alcoholics Anonymous.

On our knees before God, we present all our good, all our bad, all of our inner ugliness to Him. And when we do, we find God to be a very different God from the One we once understood. This is the God who puts His hands directly on us; the God who touches the ugliest, most hideous, most rotten parts of ourselves. This is the God who heals our wounds.

> *As we felt new power flow in, as we enjoyed peace of mind, as we discovered we could face life success-fully, as we became conscious of His presence, we began to lose our fear of today, tomorrow or the here-after. We were reborn.* (ALCOHOLICS ANONYMOUS, p. 63)

Meditation

I cannot be too unclean or too hideous for God to look at me, to touch me, to heal me. God's extravagant love is more powerful than my uncleanness.

While meditating upon the reading, pray:

One Our Father
Ten Hail Marys
One Glory be to the Father

The Fifth Healing Mystery

THE HEALING OF THE WOMAN
SUFFERING FROM HEMORRHAGE

Mark 5:21-34

When Jesus had crossed again [in the boat] to the other side, a large crowd gathered around him, and he stayed close to the sea. One of the synagogue officials, named Jairus, came forward. Seeing him he fell at his feet and pleaded earnestly with him, saying, "My daughter is at the point of death. Please, come lay your hands on her that she may get well and live." He went off with him, and a large crowd followed him and pressed upon him.

There was a woman afflicted with hemorrhages for twelve years. She had suffered greatly at the hands of many doctors and had spent all that she had. Yet she was not helped but only grew worse. She had heard about Jesus and came up behind him in the crowd and touched his cloak. She said, "If I but touch his clothes, I shall be cured." Immediately her flow of blood dried up. She felt in her body that she was healed of her affliction. Jesus, aware at once that power had gone out from him, turned around in the crowd and asked, "Who has touched my clothes?" But his disciples said to him, "You see how the crowd is pressing upon you, and yet you ask, 'Who touched me?'" And he looked around to see who had done it. The woman, realizing what had happened to her, approached in fear and trembling. She fell down before Jesus and told him the whole truth. He said to her, "Daughter, your faith has saved you. Go in peace and be cured of your affliction."

Reflection

Picture this dramatic scene: Jesus is at the center of a massive, swarming crowd. Two people are simultaneously pushing their way through this sea of humanity, both of them struggling to get near him. One is coming boldly from the front while one is coming very timidly from behind. Both feel a mixture of fear about their situation and faith in Jesus' power. Both come hoping for a healing. Before this day is over, however, both of them will experience something far beyond their wildest expectations.

The first person, a man named Jairus, is trying to attract Jesus' attention because his only daughter is dying. His fears for the life of the child he loves, coupled with his faith in Jesus, account for his presence there.

The other person is an unidentified woman anxious not to draw any attention to herself. She is actually hiding in the crowd. How do we account for her presence?

The fact is, this poor lady really shouldn't have been present in the crowd that day. Her affliction — her chronic hemorrhage — had rendered her "unclean," not worthy to be rubbing elbows with people. According to Mosaic Law, any person with an issue of body fluids was considered unclean. Therefore, anyone or anything that person touched would have been considered unclean as well.

Yes, she was "unclean," and she couldn't look people in the eye for fear they would see who and what she was. She both feared them and needed them — this crowd was her only "cover." She also both feared and needed Jesus — he was her only hope. But he mustn't see her. After all, wouldn't her uncleanness be totally offensive to his very holiness? She knew who he was, and she knew that if she could only get close enough to touch his clothing, she would be restored to full health by his healing power. So her initial plan was carefully to enter the crowd unnoticed, get within reach, touch him quickly, and escape undetected; then she would be well. She had figured it all thoroughly. She was counting on his power when she reached out.

But once her hand brushed the tassel, her plan began falling apart; things happened she hadn't counted on. Jesus had felt her touch and — oh no! Now he was asking for her! She hadn't planned on that!

At this point she probably expected to hear Jesus say punishing words, words that would rip her to shreds, and she probably wanted to run. But she didn't run. Instead she unexpectedly found herself having an honest conversation with Jesus, hearing him say words she never expected to hear — words so powerful that they reached deep inside her spirit and made her whole!

Just by his touch, this woman was already healed of her physical affliction, just as she had expected. She had felt physical power from him. But at that same moment, Jesus felt something powerful from her too: faith so strong it got his attention right in the middle of a jostling crowd!

Yet he also felt something else from her — something much worse than any physical illness. He knew she was still painfully afflicted with shame. He couldn't let her just walk away still hurting from shame. He knew that in a heart filled with shame there can be no peace — not at home alone, not in the middle of a big crowd. And so he looked at her and said these gentle, loving words of healing that she still needed to hear: "...go in peace, and be well."

The woman had counted on Jesus' power but not on his mercy. For the first time, after twelve long years of emotional pain, she would "comprehend the word serenity and she would know peace."

This true story of healing demonstrates that different people in different situations approach God from lots of different directions. It shows that our human fears are always a big part of our troubling human situations, but with faith in God, we can reach through those fears for the healing that only He can give us. Yet this is more than a good story of faith overcoming fear. It is also a story of God's extravagant love overcoming the painful shame that we in recovery always feel — the shame that can actually keep us at a distance from the only One who can heal us.

We men and women who first come into A.A. suffering from chronic alcoholism are not like Jairus; we're certainly not trying to attract God's attention. We're more like this woman. We too have come to believe in God's power to help us, and we too enter the A.A. group hoping for a miracle; yet we also approach God hiding and hoping He won't see us. Like her, we are afraid of God too. We feel so "unclean" and filled with shame that we are afraid to approach God face to face. Hiding ourselves in crowded meetings, our initial plan is often to sneak up on God from behind.

At first we're so pleased that we are now sober, that we'd easily settle for merely a physical healing, just sobriety itself. But when living sober becomes painful because we haven't yet faced the fear and shame inside us, our sponsors share with us that God desires to give us much more than just sobriety — that there are wounds inside us that still need healing. They tell us we must actively approach God for that healing through the Twelve Steps.

Those spiritual actions soon bring us to the honesty and courage of A.A.'s Step Five: "We admitted to God, to ourselves, and to another human being the exact nature of our wrongs."

Here is where we usually want to escape too. Nevertheless, we are encouraged to reach through our fears and "make ourselves completely known to him," just as this woman did. Our Fifth Step is fearfully finding ourselves having an honest conversation we never expected to have with anyone. But once we do have that talk, we are always delightfully surprised to find that God loves us so much that He doesn't want to let us walk away still hurting from shame. We reach out to God, counting on His divine power to give us sobriety, but we never really count on His divine mercy, the love of God that reaches in to heal us and make us whole.

At this powerful, healing Step, our hearts open up to hear God's gentle, loving words to us that heal the self-defeating shame that afflicts us and hurts us deep inside.

> *Once we have taken this Step, withholding nothing, we are delighted. We can look the world in the eye. We can be alone at perfect peace and ease. Our fears fall from us. We begin to feel the nearness of our Creator. We may have certain spiritual beliefs, but now we begin to have a spiritual experience. The feeling that the drink problem has disappeared will often come strongly. We feel we are on the Broad Highway, walking hand in hand with the Spirit of the Universe.*
>
> (ALCOHOLICS ANONYMOUS, p. 75)

Meditation

There can be no peace in my heart when I am still filled with shame. By God's slightest touch, by God's gentle words in my heart, the power of God's extravagant love heals the many years of shame inside me. Through the actions of Step Five, I too can "go in peace and be well."

While meditating upon the reading, pray:

> *One Our Father*
> *Ten Hail Marys*
> *One Glory be to the Father*

To end the rosary:

Pray the "Hail, Holy Queen" (for text, see p. 54).